THE GROWTH OF UNDERSTANDING
IN THE YOUNG CHILD

THE GROWTH OF UNDERSTANDING IN THE YOUNG CHILD

A Brief Introduction to Piaget's Work

NATHAN ISAACS

 Ward Lock Educational Company Limited
116, *Baker Street, London, W*.1.

© Nathan Isaacs 1961
Second impression 1963
Third impression 1964
Fourth impression 1965
Fifth impression 1966
Sixth impression 1966
Seventh impression 1968
Eighth impression 1969

7062 3263 1

Set in Monotype Bembo 12 point
Printed in Great Britain by Richard Clay (The Chaucer Press), Ltd.,
Bungay, Suffolk

CONTENTS

I

INTRODUCTION

1. The great importance of the work of Professor Jean Piaget of Geneva for child psychology, and thus for education, has only in recent years been fully recognized. This work has gone on for some thirty-five years, but the sequence of books translated between 1927 and 1932, though very stimulating, seemed open to a good many doubts. However, the volumes published in English during the last decade, and others still untranslated, have shown beyond question how much Professor Piaget can help us to understand children's intellectual growth. We owe to him a striking fresh picture of the child himself as the architect of this growth. Piaget's interest lies chiefly in the building-up of the basic framework of thought, which later the child, and we, mostly take for granted; but that is what makes the new picture so illuminating. And from the angle of Infant School teachers it is noteworthy that the period from 4-5 years to 7-8 years turns out to be a specially important one, anyway for the average run of children. For their biggest step forward in the building of that framework usually falls within this period. The present brochure will offer a thumbnail sketch of the whole story, as Piaget presents it, and will then dwell more fully on the happenings of the Infant School phase.

2. The sketch must be very "thumbnail" indeed, because of the sheer mass of Piaget's work. Since about 1935 it has been based on systematic experiments, carried out not only by Piaget himself but also by colleagues operating under his direction, and many teams of students. There are over a dozen volumes reporting experimental findings from 1935 onward, besides numerous articles by Piaget, and many semi-independent researches carried on at his Institute in recent years. Some of these volumes will be referred to later, but nothing more than sample soundings can be offered here. It is, however, worth adding that in the last few years various other workers in England have repeated sections of Piaget's investigations and mainly confirmed his results. A case of

particular interest to working teachers is that of a headmaster who read Piaget's book on the Child's Conception of Number, and, like many others, found its contents, in his own telling phrase, "either incomprehensible or incredible". However, he proceeded rightaway to try out most of the experiments in his own school, obtained the same "incredible" results and went on, in their light, to revise the school's ways of handling its arithmetic teaching. The responses were very encouraging and the experiment is going on.

3. This brings out two further points of which readers should be warned: (i) Piaget's books are in general very difficult to read; his "theory" is usually presented in a highly abstract and technical vocabulary. This is a great pity and whilst anyone undismayed by the difficulties is amply rewarded, many working teachers may well have to wait till an "Ordinary Reader's Guide to Piaget" sees the light of day. However, some few references which may prove helpful are listed on page 42. (ii) The actual experiments are usually as concrete as any child could wish and represent play situations into which even 4-5 year olds enter with ready interest. But just this fact makes the children's failures, their flat contradictions and sheer absurdities, startling to the reader who has not previously come up against these uncharted areas of small children's minds. One's first impulse is to find fault with the experiments, or anyway with this or that feature in them; but presently one notes that Piaget had foreseen one's criticisms and varied his procedure, whilst still obtaining the same results. Also a few pages later one meets children on the average only 6-12 months older who are in an obvious half-way phase, sometimes getting the easier results right, sometimes falling back into the same absurdities; whilst another 6-12 months on, the children tested are astonished at such infantile questions, and offer the answers one would expect. Moreover, as already remarked, the experiments have been independently repeated with similar results. Thus it is the very surprise-effect of Piaget's findings which measures their revealingness and shows how much new psychological understanding is to be learnt from them.

II

THE PIAGETIAN PICTURE
OF THE CHILD'S DEVELOPMENT

I. KEYS TO THE CHILD'S MENTAL GROWTH

THE MAIN KEYS to the child's mental growth, as Piaget brings them out, are (i) the paramount part played from the start by his own *action* (ii) the way this turns into a process of *inward building-up*, that is, of forming within his mind a continually extending *structure* corresponding to the world outside.

(i) *The child as agent*

(a) Piaget shows how from the beginning, the infant himself takes a controlling hand in procuring and organizing all his experience of the outside world. He follows with his eyes, explores with them, turns his head; explores with his hands, grips, lets go, pulls, pushes; explores with his mouth; moves his body and limbs; explores jointly and alternately with eye and hand, etc. All this brings experiences which come to him as the products of his activities and are formed into psychic schemes or patterns *keyed* by them. That keying becomes even more clearly marked when, happening upon an interesting experience, he is stimulated to repeat the activity that led to it, and then *goes on* with it or, after an interval, returns to it. This process of absorbing and organizing experiences round the activities that produce them Piaget calls "*assimilation*". He regards it as our most fundamental process of learning and growth, which indeed goes on for the rest of our lives. However, assimilation is always being modified by an accompanying process of *accommodation*. Many situations or objects resist the activity patterns the child tries on them, and in so doing impose some changes on these patterns themselves. Still others yield *new* results which go to enrich the range or scope of the patterns.

Thus the assimilative processes constantly extend their domain whilst at the same time accommodation steers them into ever more successful *adaptation* to the world. This dual process, and the endeavour to maintain an equal balance between the two sides, are for Piaget the chief controlling factors of intellectual growth.

(b) To begin with, the activities that organize patterns of resulting experiences round them can only be physical, directed to outward objects and situations. Their scope indeed widens all the time, as the child's powers grow and above all as he masters locomotion and his range of exploration and action is thus immensely multiplied. But in the course of the second year, these external activities also develop a great new inward dimension. Language comes in and with it a more and more settled power of evocation and representation of absent things. This power is the main foundation for the unfolding activity of thought. The latter begins essentially as a form of *action in terms of internal images*, and presently of their verbal symbols, extending the range of the child's *physical action on outward objects*. Thought is in fact for Piaget just action carried on inwardly and thus started on a new career of internal organization and growth.

(c) That story goes on developing through all the child's activities, outward and inward, during the next few years; but his most decisive advance usually comes only towards 7-8, when, by various related moves forward, he establishes himself on the level of *structured thinking*. This Piaget calls the stage of *concrete* operations of thought, because it still remains tied to tangible starting-points and goals, taken over from the real world. In the years that follow, the child exploits and consolidates these new-found powers of controlled thinking; but at the same time he prepares the ground for his next and final advance. Between 11 and 14 he attains the power of *abstract* thought—that is, thought emancipated from the given facts of the real world and able to operate freely with its own imagined possibilities and hypotheses. It can work out the logical consequences of these, or vary them or even reverse them, and draw a fresh set of consequences. How much use the child makes of this ability will depend on his bent, interests and native capacity; but in suitable subjects it can lead all the way to the most abstruse forms of logical, mathematical or scientific thought. Yet the link with action remains unbroken. All thought, as Piaget sees it, is operation, and operation is internalized action; it is this that determines the whole of our

10

human experience, all our thought-life and learning, and all human mental growth.

(ii) *The child as inward builder*

Piaget thus directs our attention to what in fact lies behind our characteristic behaviour as human beings. Right from the start we build up in our minds a kind of working model of the world around us; in other words, a model of a world of persisting and moving objects and recurring happenings set in a framework of space and time and showing a regular order. As will be described presently, Piaget shows how far this model-building is carried, in a functional yet unmistakable way, even in our first eighteen months, that is, prior to the help of language or explicit thought. Once the basic model is in our minds, the rest is merely a matter of building on, filling in and organizing; the structure remains the same, even though it is immeasurably expanded and enriched. In fact we carry it with us for the rest of our lives and although we normally take it for granted, it continually *regulates* all our planning and action. We are drawing on it—and relying upon it— whenever we start to *think out* any course of action: its space aspect when we want to get somewhere; its scheme of material objects when we want to make or construct something; its order of events, when we want to bring about or to prevent some happening.

From the appropriate part of the model in our minds we then work out the actual sequence of movements or actions which we shall have to follow. In a great number of cases this process is virtually automatic; our purposes bring into our thoughts the programmes needed to give effect to them, and we get on with these without worrying how we have come by them. If, however, we stumble on a difficulty and need to stop for some real thinking, this may well make us explicitly aware, first, of the scheme in our minds which has carried us so far, secondly of the nature of the present gap in it, and thirdly of what help we might be able to get from bringing further parts of our thought-resources to bear.

If then we consider the whole range of planned courses of action on which we constantly launch ourselves, we can get some measure of the connected and organized scheme of things in our minds on which they must rest. Our plans of course always contemplate the real world itself, in which they are to be realized; but the point is that when we are making them, we are *foreseeing*, *forethinking* and *foreplanning*, and can therefore only be doing so from the model of that real world in our *minds*. We are naturally thinking of the real world, but at that stage we are only *thinking* of it. However our model so truly corresponds to it, at any rate in its main structure, that we can pass straight over from the model to the real world without any further thought. It is only in matters of comparative detail that it is liable to prove wrong or insufficient.

Piaget's work can greatly help us to grasp this situation, since it shows more clearly than anything before just how we build up that structured model of the world in our minds. We are not born with it, but have to construct it piecemeal, right from its foundations. Piaget demonstrates in detail how the child does this, from the first few weeks of his life onward. Here is the briefest outline of the process as he exhibits it.

2. THE MAIN BUILDING STAGES

(i) *First 18 months; sensori–motor phase*

Through a series of revealing tests on his own three infants, Piaget brings out the stages by which the first building up proceeds. The earliest behaviour shows not the least sense of persisting objects or of the most rudimentary space or time relations. But presently it is seen to change, and month by month it takes more account of these features of the world, until the child clearly has in his mind a scheme that corresponds to them. We see him *recognizing* different objects as such and expecting them to persist, to move in space and to display spatial characters and relations. Similarly he *recognizes* different happenings and expects them to take a certain course, expects some of them to lead on to others, and so on. The infant's conduct is now visibly *pre*-adjusted to all this; i.e. it is controlled by something in his mind which regularly anticipates just those features. How he is led to form that controlling schema has already been referred to; he learns by doing and trying, by assimilating all the different experiences that thus come to him, and by constantly varying and extending his experimental activities. And by eighteen months the range and variety of his

12

purposive behaviour already bears witness to the controlling presence in his mind of the sort of basic world-model I have described.

(ii) *18 months to 4-5 years: stage of intuitive thought*

So much having already been achieved, the child has only to go on to exploit all the further instruments and powers that come to him. He now incessantly expands and enriches, works over, organizes and re-organizes, his inward model of the world. He does so mainly through imaginative play on the one hand and through more exploring and experimenting, combined with questioning, listening and talking, on the other hand. The different kinds of objects and happenings which he can recognize, pre-adjust to, remember and imagine continually increase, whilst at the same time his sense of space-relations and time-relations becomes more varied and better articulated. Yet most of the detailed images and ideas in his mind tend to remain vague and unstable, and his thinking cannot move away from present situations without losing itself.

(iii) *4-5 years to 7-8 years: advance to stage of concrete operations*

Piaget now concentrates above all on the state of the child's main *frame-work* notions and what happens to them. Thus he examines how children progress in their notions of different aspects of space, of time, of movement and speed, of number and measure, and of elementary logical relations such as those of whole and part, classes and sub-classes, or serial order, etc. By numerous experiments he shows that most 4-5 year olds of average intelligence have as yet no settled notions in any of these fields. Everything is still in a state of flux, nothing is clear or stays put. Size, shape, arrangement, etc. are mixed up with number; distance and length with movement; rate of movement with overtaking or catching up; time with speed, and so on.

The same experiments, however, carried out with children only about a year older show the *beginnings* of a notable change. At least in the simpler cases they can, by trial and error, sort their ideas out, and thus get some first inklings of the true meaning of distance, length, number and the rest. Thereafter there is usually further piecemeal progress and then, perhaps another year on, the scene is transformed. By 7-8 years children deal with most of the concrete experimental situations much as an ordinary adult would. Each of the basic structural concepts is now clear and stable. In Piaget's language, the level of "conservation" has been reached. That is, distance, length, number, speed, mass, class-inclusion, etc., now each stand for something *constant*, whichever way round it is taken, however it is sub-divided, and, in the case of number, however it is arranged in space, concentrated or spread. Moreover we have here concepts that can be linked together in larger structures which in turn have the same character of conservation. In fact various sets of these concepts taken together come to form distinctive schemes of operational thought. That means, schemes of connected relational *reasoning*, either mathematical or logical, such as eventually make up geometry, arithmetic, mathematics at large, mechanics, and the formal logical aspects of all other sciences. That may seem to be looking a long way ahead, and is not properly realized till the stage of full abstract reasoning is reached at 11-14 years. What Piaget establishes, however, is that the first prototypes of these operational ideas, that is, concepts that possess the minimum characters needed, are present in most children's minds from the age of 7-8 years. Thus the basic structure of their world is now properly laid down in their thought, not of course in words, but in functioning ideas. Therefore they can think out, flexibly and successfully, the simple everyday space relations (distances, sizes, etc.), time-relations (intervals, successions, overlaps, etc.), or mechanical, numerical and logical relations which we all continually need. How far they have had to travel in order to get to this level is shown in the most illuminating way by Piaget's work on the earlier stages, from about 4-5 years onward.

III

THE CONCEPT OF NUMBER

All this long struggle forward in children's thinking comes out very clearly in the development of their number ideas—the part of Piaget's work which is now best known in this country. It offers a striking illustration both of the nature of his discoveries and of the basic pattern of mental growth. We can watch how the child starts from a level of utter confusion, without a notion of what number really means even though he may be able to count to ten or twenty; a level where number is completely mixed up with size, shape and arrangement, or constantly shifts according to the way it is subdivided or added up. And we can see how, on an average two years later, children declare of their own accord that a number *must* stay the same, whatever you do with it, so long as you do not actually add to it or take away from it; or that whatever you have done with it, you can always reverse this and get back to where you started from; or that you can always show it to be the same by counting; and so on.

The following are a few examples of the ways in which Piaget's experiments bring out this pattern of growth:

1. Each child was presented with *two* vessels of the same shape and size containing equal quantities of coloured liquid. Then the contents of one of them was poured into (a) two similar but smaller vessels, (b) several such, (c) a tall but narrow vessel, (d) a broad but shallow one. In each case the child was asked whether the quantity of liquid was still the same as in the untouched vessel.

Piaget found that at a first stage, around 4-5 years, children took it for granted that the quantity of liquid was now *different*—either more because the level was higher, or more because there were more glasses, or less because the new vessel was narrower, or less because the levels in the two or more glasses were lower. In other words, there was no idea of a constant quantity, independent of its changing forms; if its appearance changed, the quantity changed and could become either more or less according to what aspect of the new appearance caught the child's eye. At a second stage, at about 5½–6, children had reached a transitional phase, in which they wavered uncertainly between the visual appearances and the dawning idea of conservation in their minds. Thus the quantity of liquid might be regarded as still the same when it was poured into *two* smaller glasses, but as greater when it was poured into *three*. Or as remaining the same if the difference in level or cross-section in the new vessel was small, but not if it was larger. Or the child might *try* to allow for the relation between cross-section and level, and experiment uncertainly without reaching any clear conclusion. In the third stage, between 6½ and 8, children give the correct answers right away, either by reference to the height-width relation, or by pointing out that the quantity has not been changed: "It's only been poured out".

2. As a check on these results, Piaget carried out a similar set of experiments, with beads instead of liquids. In this way something close to counting could be introduced (e.g. the child putting beads into a container one by one as the experimenter did the same into another vessel). Also he could be asked to imagine that the beads inside each vessel were arranged into the familiar shape of a necklace. The outcome was entirely the same. At the first stage, the children thought that the quantity of beads would be either more or less, and would make a longer or shorter necklace, according as the level looked higher, or the width greater, or there were more vessels, and this happened even when a child had put one bead into his vessel for each one that the experimenter placed in his. At stage 2 there is a struggle in the child's mind as before. This may show itself for example by his first going wrong when comparing levels between a wider and a taller vessel; then correcting himself if asked to think in terms of the necklaces; but when the beads are spread over two or more containers, still thinking that the necklace will be longer. At stage 3 once more the children reply correctly and cannot be shaken, however the questions or the experiments may be varied.

3. The next experiments were intended to test whether children could match two sets of objects against one another, and could then *hold on* to this equality as something conserved or constant. Thus they were asked to tally eggs with egg-cups, bottles with glasses, vases with flowers, or to buy so many flowers with so many coins at a flower per coin.

For example, six small bottles were put on a table and the child was offered a tray of say 10 glasses and asked to place a glass by each bottle. The 4-5 year olds at stage 1 took an arbitrary number of glasses, or all of them, and even then, through arranging them much closer together than the bottles, concluded that there were more bottles than glasses. At stage 2 (up to about 6 years) the matching gave no difficulty, but if the experimenter brought the glasses closer together than the bottles, the children found more bottles than glasses. If then the glasses were spread out further, they found more of these than bottles. They could not be shifted from these beliefs, whatever changes were rung on the situation, including even getting a child to count off, first six bottles and then six glasses. At stage 3 (illustrated here by one child of $5\frac{1}{2}$ and another of 6; 2) the right answer is given at once, whatever the experimenter does, and he is told that he has "only put the bottles close together", etc.

The flower-and-vase and eggcup-and-egg experiment proved somewhat easier because the children were more used to matching these objects; but apart from rather quicker progress, the character of the responses was much the same.

The exchange of flowers for coins one by one presented no difficulties even at stage 1. But when it was completed and the coins put in a row whilst the flowers were bunched—or else the flowers in a row and the coins piled up—there were either more coins than flowers or more flowers than coins. At stage 2 the sole progress was that children no longer had to proceed one by one, but could match four coins against four flowers, or seven against seven. But the moment the visual correspondence was disturbed, the equivalence was lost again. At stage 3 (one case as young as 4; 11) equality was firmly insisted upon, whatever the visual appearance, either because it could be restored by matching, or because once it had been created, it was *there* ("Because I gave you my pennies").

4. As another test of a similar order, children were presented with various patterns formed from counters, and asked to pick out of a box the same number of counters. The patterns chosen were (a) a random array, (b) two parallel rows, (c) closed figures like a circle or a house, (d) closed figures based on a fixed small number of counters, e.g. a square, a cross, etc., (e) more complex and less familiar figures, like a rhombus.

At stage 1 there are only what Piaget calls "global qualitative comparisons", or "rough reproductions of the configuration of the models". At stage 2 the children still try to reproduce the model, but now do so counter for counter. However, if the resulting shape is changed, equality vanishes, though they have themselves just established it on a one to one basis. At stage 3 they no longer depend on reproducing the figures, but if necessary break these up and arrange them in a series, to make sure that they arrive at the right number of counters.

By way of a further variant of these tests, children were shown a row of six beans, representing sweets or coins, and asked to pick the same number from a pile. Here again the stage 1 subjects go by either the length of the row, or its density, but have no thought of co-ordinating the two. Thus a child might put down 10 beans as equal to 6, then notice that the 10 made a shorter row and add some more. If the 6 were spread out further, he would keep adding, but if they were closed up and his new row spread out, he would say "Now *I* have more" ... On the other hand there were those who went by the density and thought that 6 were more than 7 "because they're close together; there are a lot". At stage 2 the children could get as far as picking the correct number and setting it over against the model, but if either row was then spaced out or closed up, the equality would again be denied. At stage 3 the right number is picked and placed in a shorter or longer row, or just heaped up, without any regard for what is done to the model.

5. Experiments to test whether children have grasped the arithmetical relation of parts to a whole, or of equal parts:

(i) They were handed four beans to represent four sweets for the morning break, and another four intended for tea-time. After that two more lots of four were put in front of them and they were told that these were for tomorrow, but they would only eat one in the morning and save all the others for tea-time. As they watched, three sweets would be taken away from one of these sets and added to the other. The children would then be asked to compare the two (4 + 4 and 1 + 7), and say whether they would be eating the same number tomorrow as to-day. At stage 1 they will consider 7 + 1 either more or less than 4 + 4, according as they compare the 7 or the 1 with the 4's in the other group, but they will not see them as equal. At stage 2 children begin the same way, but gradually realize that although 7 is greater than 4, there is also 1 which is less than 4 and that this should act as a set-off. At stage 3 that is now self-evident. The members of each set have become units, which, however grouped, make up the same total, since one set grows as the other shrinks. Addition and subtraction are now *understood*.

(ii) Two unequal groups of counters (8 and 14) were shown and the children asked to make them equal by shifting units from one to the other (combined addition and subtraction). At stage 1 they just take some from the larger set and add them to the other, or else keep moving counters backward and forward, with an eye only on the smaller lot, and no idea that increasing the one means decreasing the other. At stage 2 children think up the notion of arranging the counters in comparable figures, say circles, with a few in the middle, but if the figure is altered in any way, the equality they have themselves established vanishes again. At stage 3 they deliberately pair off the counters and then divide the difference.

(iii) Children were asked to share out a heap of counters equally between two people. At stage 1, they would make a rough division, but though this might chance to be right, they would think it wrong if one lot took up more space than the other. Or they might even deal out the counters one by one, and still think the two lots unequal if one looked larger or smaller. At stage 2, they would expressly build up two matching rows (or other figures) but again deny this equality as soon as the spacing was altered. At stage 3 they would share out their counters one or two at a time into equal sets, and no re-arrangement could put them off, because they had "put the same on both sides".

The foregoing covers only a limited part of the test situations described in "The Child's Conception of Number". Besides others dealing with cardinal numbers, there is an interesting sequence concerned with serial arrangements, and with ordinal numbers and their relation to cardinal ones. There are also tests of children's understanding of the *logical* relation between a whole and its parts, as distinct from the *arithmetical* one, but bringing out the close kinship of the two. The main aim of the entire volume is to demonstrate what it takes for children to get the *real meaning* of number, that is, to separate this out from shape and size, spacing and arrangement and to place it in its own distinctive realm. That realm is one in which—as the child has to discover—each number conserves its own character, however much it may be taken apart and then put together again differently, or however it may be subdivided or grouped and re-grouped. But at the same time all the numbers belong together in one number scheme and are made up by the same operations. These operations of counting and adding and subtracting (and, later, their more complicated and powerful forms: multiplying and dividing) can be combined at will, taken in any order, and above all, they can always be "done the other way round", or *reversed*. That (as the child finds) is the very nature of the relation between addition and subtraction, and similarly between multiplication and division. In fact, it lies behind the persistence or conservation of all the separate numbers, each of which can be thought of as a permanent junction point for a different set of combining or balancing operations.

This is the kind of operational notion of number which the child has to achieve—and which, on the average between about 6½ and 8 years, he does attain, anyway for those lower numbers that he can easily handle in his mind. In ordinary children of 4-5, there is not a trace of such a notion (even though they may be able to count freely to 10 or even 20); and any attempt to convey it to them meets with blank incomprehension or firm rejection. At an average age of 5-6 there are only tentative beginnings, and some first ability to respond to reiterated suggestions or promptings. Yet in children only 1-2 years older the whole basic idea is there. On the lower number level (that is, where the child does not get lost among unfamiliar symbols), he can now handle the various numerical relations as the situation demands. He can see, for example, how a number like 12 can be split up in the most various ways and yet stays the same 12 all the way through. And he can sweep aside all the non-numerical irrelevancies, like spacing, shape, size, etc. which a year or two earlier so confused him and defeated his number sense. The idea of number and all the operations connected with it now forms in fact an organized scheme in his mind under a single control.

Of course this remains a functional or working achievement, not a verbal one. The child can correctly *use* the notion of number and bring to bear the relations he needs, but he would not be able to put into formal words the principles that direct his practice. That, however, is not the important thing. Indeed, these principles—the "conservation of number", or "associativity", or "reversibility"—would mean nothing, if expressed in these terms, even to good arithmeticians among ordinary adults. What does matter is that the child's real grasp of the "number" idea will usually be limited to the figures he is familiar with in daily life, and there will be little or nothing to link up this grasp with his school arithmetic. For that most often only consists for him in a lot of "rules", mechanically learnt and not at all digested or understood; and he may never get beyond that stage. Whereas of course the *object* of his school arithmetic should be to make all the rules, and all the more complicated ways of handling numbers, *grow* out of his own grasp of the underlying idea. If that were to be the aim, the very first task would clearly be to help the child to master this *idea* (in terms naturally of the easy small numbers). For that purpose no time or trouble would be too much, and there would be no thought of going further until it was accomplished.

That brings me to the threshold of what Piaget's findings imply for education. Before I turn to this theme, however, let me try to illustrate very briefly the range of his work on some of our other main "framework" ideas.

IV

CHILDREN'S BASIC NOTIONS ABOUT
SPACE, MOVEMENT AND TIME

I CAN ONLY GIVE a few simplified *samples*, since on the subject of space alone Piaget has two large volumes of experimental investigations, whilst "Movement and Speed" and "Time" fill two more books (as yet untranslated).

I. THE NOTION OF DISTANCE

Two dolls or toy trees of equal height are placed 50 cm. away from one another. (i) A cardboard screen, slightly higher, is set up between them and the children are asked whether the original figures are still as near one another, or as far apart, as they were before. (ii) They are also asked whether it is as far (or near) from the first figure to the second as from the second to the first. The experiment is varied by making one of the figures twice the height of the other, and again by raising one of them some 50 cm. above the level of the other.

At stage 1 (4-5 years), if the questions are understood, the screen is sometimes thought to bring the two figures nearer to one another, but most often the child just substitutes the distance to the screen for the total distance between the figures.

In his reply to the second question, he thinks the distance greater one way than the other because the second doll is "far away", or is "taller" or "high up".

At stage 2 (5-7 years) there is a first phase in which the distance is no longer broken up by the screen, but is thought to be shortened to the extent of its thickness. Furthermore, it still tends to be regarded as greater in one direction than in the other.

In a later phase, there are two intermediate responses: (i) the distance may now be the same when reckoned from either end, but if a screen is interposed, this still alters it; (ii) the screen no longer affects it, but it still varies according to the end from which it is taken, especially if one figure is higher than the other. Either way, the notion of distance as such, based on a single containing space, is not achieved yet; it still turns on the standpoint of the speaker, what he is seeing, the effort he would have to make, etc.

At stage 3 (from 7 years onward) the questions are at once correctly answered and distance is not affected by interpolated objects, by the direction in which it is measured, or by any other extraneous factor.

2. NOTION OF LENGTH

(i) Children have before them a horizontal straight stick and underneath it a length of wavy plasticine with its two ends in line with those of the stick. They have to say whether these are the same length or whether one is longer than the other.

At stage 1, up to 4½ years, most of the children are positive that the length is the same. This applies even after they have been invited to follow the windings of the plasticine "snake" with their fingers. Furthermore when it is straightened out for them, they see it to be longer, but the moment it is bent into wave shape again, they once more call the length the same. In one case a child begins by saying that the "snake" is *shorter*, because it is "twisted", but after seeing it to be actually *longer*, he decides, when it is bent again, that the two lengths are the same.

At the beginning of stage 2 (4½-5 years) children still, for a start, consider only the end-points and judge the two lengths equal. However when they follow the winding line with their fingers, or are asked to picture somebody walking along it, they see that it is longer (though they may presently go back to their original judgment). By the end of stage 2 (5½-7 years) they straighten the "snake" out themselves in their minds and thus discover its greater length.

(ii) Children are shown two straight rods of say 5 cm. each, with their ends in line, and have no difficulty in seeing that they are the same length. One is then moved to project 1-2 cm. beyond the other, and they are asked which is longer, or whether they are the same length.

At stage 1 (4½-6 years) the projecting rod is found longer, and one five-year-old, when the relation of the two rods has been reversed, holds that they are *both* longer. (Length is identified with "reaching further"; the projection is followed with the eye and only the projecting end is attended to.)

At stage 2 (5-7½ years) there is every sort of intermediate re-action, shifting of ground, indecision, etc., but the correct answer gradually prevails. (A child of 6; 10 says that if one looks at one rod, that seems longer, but if at the other rod, then that one. However, when he is asked "And if one looks at both", he re-plies "Then it's the same thing" and sticks to this.)

At stage 3 (6½-7½ years) the child at once gives the right reply for the right reasons (pointing to the space left unoccupied; or remarking that one rod projects one way, the other the other way, or that one rod has just been *shifted*; or commenting "still the same, the rods can't grow!")

3. THE NOTION OF AN AREA

To test children's grasp of this notion, a situation is devised in which equal areas are subtracted from equal areas and the child has to say whether the spaces left over are the same.

Two rectangular cardboard sheets, about 20 × 30 cm., are coloured green to represent two fields. Each has by its side a wooden cow which will be eating the grass. The child recognizes that the two cows will have the same amount of grass to eat. A wooden house is put down in the *middle* of one field, so that one cow has less grass than the other, but another house of the same size is now placed in a *corner* of the other field, and the question is put whether the two cows have the same amount of grass again. More houses are put down, one for one, in each field, but in the first they are scattered over the middle, whilst in the second they are put close to each other in the same corner. The child has to say each time whether the cows still have the same amount of grass, and this may be continued till there are 15 to 20 houses in each field; children have been found to reply "yes" up to 14 houses each, and then suddenly to fail because the visual difference has become too big for them.

At stage 1 not enough interest can usually be aroused for the experiment to continue. At stage 2a (5-5½ years) children are sure that the amount of grass left is *not* the same, from the first two houses onward. This may happen even if at first both are put down in the middle, and then, after the child has agreed that this leaves the cows with the *same* amount of grass, one of the houses is shifted to the corner of its field. As soon as this is done, he is certain that the cow feeding there now has *more* grass. Other children fail when there are two houses apiece, yet others with three apiece, and so on. If an attempt is made to prove to a child that equal spaces remain over, by showing him how two like sets of small cubes will exactly cover the two green areas left, he has his own answer. Though he had seen for himself that the two sets of cubes exactly matched each other, he now considers that the cubes, too, are no longer the same number.

At stage 2b (6-7 years) children have the right idea, but begin to waver if the visual contrast becomes too great.

At stage 3 (7-8 years) they are quite sure of their ground and will point out that there is the same number of houses in each case. If the questions are continued, they regard this as a joke. Or they may themselves remark that the amount of grass left looks different, but must be equal in each field, because an equal number of houses has been put in each.

4. THE NOTIONS OF LINEAR AND CIRCULAR ORDER

(i) *Reproducing a linear order*

Children are shown a rod with 7 or 9 beads of different colours threaded on it. They are then asked to pick out a similar set from a larger number of beads in front of them, and to arrange these along another rod in the same colour order. Or there is a "clothes line" with 7 or 9 pieces of "washing" hanging from it, and they are given another on which to hang a similar set in the same order, again taken from a larger array.

(ii) *Turning a circular into a linear order*

Children are shown a circular necklace formed by 7-9 differently coloured beads and are asked to arrange another set in the same colour order along a straight rod.

(iii) *Reversing the order*

The children are invited to carry out the foregoing operations in the reverse order.

(iv) *Stacking in direct and reverse order*

The "washing" is to be taken off the two lines and stacked in two baskets. In one case the child is to start at the left hand end, in the other at the right hand end, and whilst he is doing this, he is asked to say whether he can foresee what is going to follow what.

(v) *Reproducing a figure of eight*

Children are invited to copy a set of beads disposed in a figure of eight, either on a flexible wire which can be bent into the same figure, or on a rigid rod.

At stage 1a (3–3½ years) children can pick out the right colours or items, but have no idea of order. At stage 1b (3½–4 years) *pairs* begin to appear, at first only after a little prompting, but later also spontaneously.

At stage 2a (4½–6 years) children can reproduce the direct order, provided they can keep comparing and can put each bead, etc. under the corresponding one in the model. If this is shifted to one side, they fail. The circular and reverse orders are beyond their scope. The relation "between" is not understood yet.

At stage 2b (5–6 years) the direct order can be reproduced without the help of visual correspondence, and circular order can be translated into linear; but no reverse order can be constructed yet.

After an intermediate phase of trial and error, the child reaches stage 3 (6½–7½ years) where he can construct an inverse order by direct reversible thinking, without needing to grope or feel his way. The figure of eight or a widely spaced series may still present a little difficulty, but this is very quickly mastered.

5. THE NOTION OF ORDER AS APPLIED TO MOVING BODIES

Three beads or dolls, A–B–C, joined together, are passed through a cardboard tunnel. The questions put are (i) in what order will they come out at the other end, (ii) if they go back through the tunnel, in what order will they come out then. (iii) The child is made to sit on the other side of the table and asked the first question again. (iv) The beads or dolls having again entered the tunnel (in the original order A–B–C), this is then turned through 180° in front of the child, who has to say in what order they will now come out, at the same point. (v) The same question is put after *two* turns of 180.° (vi) The experimenter keeps on making these turns, first an odd and then an even number of times, and repeats his question each time. (vii) If a child has never claimed of his own accord that the middle object B would come out first, the tunnel is given a random number of 180° turns and he is invited to say which he thinks might come out first, A or B or C? If he replies "B" he is asked how this could happen. (The beads or dolls will only just go into the tunnel, so that B clearly cannot be pushed over the top of A or C.)

The above questions may also be put about 4 or 5 objects, and not merely three.

At stage 1 (4-5½ years) children can only answer (i) correctly. They assume that the reverse order will be the same as the direct, and even when the opposite is shown to them, they are unable to "learn" this fact in the sense of thereafter foreseeing it. In some instances, moreover, they may make the middle object come out first, even though they have previously seen that B cannot move out of its "in-between" position.

At stage 2a (5½-7½ years) they succeed with the straight reversal (ii) but with nothing more, anyway to begin with. At 2b (almost the same age-range) children manage (iii) and (iv) without difficulty, but have to fall back on trial and error for (v) and (vi). By this time, if there are only the three beads or dolls, the child can see that B must stay in the middle; but if there are five, he is still apt to suppose that perhaps one of those in between might come out first.

At stage 3 (6½-7½ years) the children straightaway give all the right answers for the right reasons.

6. THE NOTION OF DISTANCES TRAVELLED

The children are offered a board on which two lengths of string mark out two "tramway tracks". One forms a straight line, the other turns right and left in equal rectangular segments, and they start and end in alignment with one another.

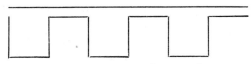

A bead representing a tram passes along each route. The experimenter's "tram" travels along several of the rectangular segments and he invites the children to make their "trams" go an equally long way along the straight track. If a child lets his "tram" stop exactly opposite the experimenter's, he suggests their going back to the station together, that is, the child's "tram" keeping level with his on the straight track, while he goes back segment by segment. This will mean that the child gets back first, and he can then be asked how this could happen. He is also offered a cardboard strip and told that perhaps he could use it to see whether the two tracks really are the same length.

At stage 1a (5½-6 years) children go entirely by the points of arrival. If these are in line, the same distance has been covered, and no proofs to the contrary can move them away from this belief. At stage 1b (5½-6½ years) judicious questions, and also what happens on the return journey, can bring the child round to the right view for a short time, but if the experiment is continued, he will tend to return to his first idea.

At stage 2a (5½-7½ years) he begins as in stage 1 but, helped by the discussion, he presently succeeds in detaching the notion of distances travelled from that of points of arrival. At 2b (6-7 years) he attends from the start to the actual lengths of the two routes, but is unable yet to do any measuring; the strip offered to him is rejected or disregarded, or else only applied in a random way.

At stage 3 (7-8½ years) he goes on to actual measurement, at first with some fumbling, later with full assurance.

7. THE NOTION OF SPEED

(i) *The speed of two movements where only their end-points are seen*

Two dolls are passed through two straight tunnels, one 55 cm., the other 40 cm. long. They leave and arrive at the same moment, and the child is asked whether one of them went faster than the other. If he fails with this, he is shown what happens, without the tunnels, so that he can see one of the dolls going faster than the other. The tunnel performance is then repeated and the same question is put to him again.

At stage 1 (5-6 years) the child insists that the two dolls went equally fast because they arrived together, and nothing can persuade him otherwise. Even though he has watched one moving faster than the other outside the tunnel, this, when no longer seen, is overruled by simultaneous arrival, which he *translates* into "moving equally fast".

At stage 2 (around 6 years) the child begins with the same idea but gradually works up to the right conclusion.

At stage 3 (6½-7½ years) the time and space relations are all *reasoned* out correctly right away.

(ii) *Fully visible movements, with common starting-points.*

1. The children have before them a drawing of a straight horizontal road AB and another, AC, which diverges from this. They can see that AC is longer than AB and are told that two cars will be starting along them at the same time and going equally fast. Will one arrive before the other? Later on they are shown what happens and asked why the car going along AC arrived at C *after* the other had reached B. (2) The same questions are based on a straight and a winding road going from A to B. (3) The two cars travelling along AB and AC now leave A together and arrive at the same time, one at B and the other at C. Has one gone faster than the other? What happens is then actually shown and the children are again asked to say whether the speeds were the same or different. (4) A similar sequence of questions is put about cars leaving together along the two roads, one straight, one winding, leading from A to B.

At stage 1 (5-6 years) the children expect the two cars, in the case of both (1) and (2), to arrive at the same time. When shown that one arrives earlier they insist that it went quicker, though they had been told that the cars were travelling equally fast. In cases (3) and (4), if the cars arrive at the same time, they must be moving at the same speed, even when the contrary has just been shown. Occasionally, however, a child will say in case (4) that the car along the straight road went faster because it was a shorter road. All the contradictory facts are explained away on grounds such as one car having been pushed, or not having gone fast enough, or both having gone very slowly. Neither the idea of speed, nor that of time taken, nor that of true distance, have been mastered yet. Greater speed means overtaking; if there is no overtaking, speeds cannot be compared, or else are the same.

At stage 2a (5½-7½ years) there is success with (1) and (2); the time taken is now seen to go with the lengths of the two roads, which no longer depend on the coincidence or alignment of their end-points. In (3) and (4), however, involving speed proper, the children fail, even after they have watched the actual facts. At stage 2b (6½–7½ years) there is a gradual realization of the right answers to (3) and (4), but only after the true facts have been demonstrated.

At stage 3 (7–8 years) the three ideas of length of road, length of time and speed are from the outset correctly related and structured.

8. THE NOTION OF TIME: SUCCESSION, DURATION AND SIMULTANEITY

A race is played out on a table by means of two small dolls which are made to advance at different speeds and by separate spurts along parallel tracks. The following questions are then put:

(i) Doll No. 1 goes from A to D, whilst doll No. 2 goes from A to B, and No. 1 then stops, whilst No. 2 goes from B to C. The child who has watched this is asked which stopped first. Or No. 1 is supposed to stop at midday, and the question takes the form: did No. 2 stop before or after midday?

(ii) Did No. 1 and No. 2 run the same length of time, or as long as each other, or if not, which went on a longer time?

(iii) If No. 1 stops at C and No. 2 *simultaneously* at B, the child is asked whether they stopped at the same moment or not, and if not, which stopped first.

These questions can be readily varied, e.g. different departure times, but simultaneous halts, or different starting points, but simultaneous halts at the same place, etc.

At stage 1 (4½–5 years) none of the time relations are yet distinguished from the spatial ones: "a longer time" means "farther"; "first" or "sooner" means "in front of" or sometimes "behind". There is no strict simultaneity, and duration is proportional to distance travelled. The child may consider that No. 1 took a longer time than No. 2 *because* it moved faster, or that No. 2 stopped sooner *because* it did not go so far. There are continual contradictions and changes of mind. Correct replies occur side by side with wrong ones and many of the answers appear just random.

At stage 2a (5–6½ years) time order and space order are beginning to separate out, though still very imperfectly. There may be progress with the idea of succession, but not with that of duration;

or vice versa. Neither simultaneity nor coinciding durations may be grasped yet, or only one but not the other. At stage 2b ($6\frac{1}{2}$–$7\frac{1}{2}$ years) succession and duration are brought into relation and, with some help from the experimenter, the child gets his first proper hold both on the idea of simultaneity and on that of coinciding durations. However, a return to the old confusions may still occur.

At stage 3 (7–$8\frac{1}{2}$ years) time and space are at length fully sorted out. Succession in time is now clearly distinguished from spatial order, and co-ordinated with duration and with simultaneity in a single, reversible system. The child can deduce the correct reply to each question directly from this coherent scheme of time-relations in his mind.

V

EDUCATIONAL BEARINGS OF PIAGET'S WORK

1. WE SHOULD NOTE first of all that whilst Piaget's studies of the earliest years cover the whole basic pattern of learning, later he deals almost solely with *structural* growth, the framework concepts of space, time, number, and so on. We must thus distinguish between the more general bearings of his psychology as a whole, and what his *structural* enquiries imply for the specific education of children in arithmetic, geometry and related fields. There is of course no inconsistency between the two; the latter are a special case of the former. Both merit our most careful attention; the first for educational theory and practice at large, the second for some of its most troublesome applications. Both will be briefly reviewed below; but before doing this, we must clear out of the way a double misunderstanding of Piaget's findings, which often hinders their true assessment.

On the one hand his results have been taken to refer to the processes of native growth, or inward *maturation*, of the child's mind. On the other hand, they have been held to establish—or to claim to establish—the actual *age* to which each stage of this maturation is tied. Thus, on such an interpretation, children of 4-5 would be incapable of the idea of number, or of most spatial ideas, or of certain elementary logical ones, etc. Those of about 6 would only just be able to grope their way forward in very easy cases. One would, in fact, have to wait till about 7-8 before one could expect any real grasp of even apparently simple numerical, spatial, temporal or logical relations. This then, if valid, seems to call for drastic re-thinking of much of the work of all our ordinary Infant Schools; but it seems to set a barrier also to what the most "active" and progressive methods can do for children under 7-8.

However, as already said, all this is but a misunderstanding, even if it has been fostered at times by some of Piaget's own ways of presenting his results. Careful consideration of his work as a whole shows how mistaken is such a reading. First, as regards the relation of age and stage Piaget claims nothing more than that the ranges he cites represent his actual findings on the Genevan school-children who were tested. We find in fact that the ranges given are very wide, besides being mere averages. Furthermore, his detailed figures plainly show a large *overlap* between the stages. Thus some 4-5 year olds produce replies characteristic of the 7-8 average, and some 7-8's respond like average 4-5's. Piaget has himself insisted that his age-ranges are no more than a useful framework of reference for the way in which the stages *succeed* one another; it is the order of succession that matters, and not any particular chronological age.

On the other point, the apparent heavy stress on maturation, the answer is simply that what Piaget is setting out to study is not the differences which different environments might make, but the *common* stages and laws of *all* children's mental growth. There is enough scope in such a study to keep any investigator fully engaged without his going outside that task. This does not, however, mean *denying* the influence of outward factors, or treating mental growth as resulting only from inward maturation. On the contrary, Piaget's whole psychology rests on the principle of continuous *interaction* between the child and the world around him; it is this that furnishes all the material, as well as the motive force, for his intellectual advance. Thus there can be no question for Piaget of any purely internal process of development irrespective of the quality of the environment.

He would hold, of course, like most of us, that the way our human minds grow is at bottom prescribed by our human endowment and capacities, so that if growth goes on at all, it must assume certain characteristic forms. It is these in which he is most interested and on which he concentrates. But on his own premises one would expect that favourable or unfavourable outward conditions would bear strongly on the success and extent of development. The former might go far to promote it; the latter to arrest or warp it. Piaget would certainly have the utmost sympathy with any enquiry that aimed at establishing the *optimum* setting for mental growth. He might indeed well consider that his own findings pointed to what that setting should be, even though it was not for him as a psychologist, but rather for teachers, to work out the practical implications.

These implications do not in fact diminish the teacher's powers

33

and responsibilities in any way, nor do they in the least support any attitude of just waiting whilst the child inwardly matures. The *order* of stages in mental growth is what Piaget is concerned to make clear; but whether they will be passed through with greater or less speed or zest or all-round gain, or whether the later stages will be reached at all, is a wide-open question. From that angle, it may be vitally important whether the educator has or has not provided the right conditions and help for the child.

2. This brings us directly to the light thrown on these conditions by Piaget's own new psychological picture of intellectual growth. Here we can first of all say broadly that what his psychology does is to supply a solid new foundation and a fresh weight and authority for just those pregnant insights which we already owe to the great educational reformers of the past. That of course becomes very clear, once the false "maturational" interpretation is corrected, but the actual elements of this new accession of strength to "active" education merit a special glance.

(i) First and foremost, Piaget brings out all the *psychological* gulf between the true learning that is growth and the so-called learning which is mere verbal training, habit formation, or the mechanical mastery of skills and knacks. The former is our great human achievement, which starts practically from birth and in some degree goes on all our lives. Its main motor throughout is the child's own active doing, and learning from doing. Above all else, it is *cumulative*. That is, it forms a structure in the child's mind which he himself keeps building up. Each new level is only made possible by what has been built before, but then leads on to a further advance, and a greater and richer whole. The second kind of learning, on the other hand, has real value only as far as it provides *working means and tools* for the first type. If treated as an end in itself (whatever show it may make) it becomes worthless. Verbal "learning" can be "taught" by drilling and cramming at any time, but tends to be shed almost as soon as the cramming stops. Moreover, if it remains merely verbal, it is only a meaningless "act", even while it lasts. To *some* extent, of course, it can join up under favourable conditions with the "real" learning that goes on all the time, and to that extent it achieves true value; but how little that amounts to among average school children is only too lamentably plain.

(ii) True learning is learning not only by doing but also by

34

understanding. That however again means *genuine* understanding, which is intimately linked with doing and largely dependent upon this. As already emphasized, the child constructs in his mind in his first 18 months a basic working model of the world which he can then use for the assimilation of all his new experiences. That assimilation to what he already firmly holds is what brings the sense of understanding to him.

In the course of these further assimilations the original model is itself constantly extended and further filled in. At the same time its content is being sorted and grouped and *ordered* in diverse ways, by various kinds of likenesses and relationships. Furthermore, as "accommodation" operates, and shortcomings and errors come to light, the model gets revised and, where necessary, re-organized. Thus if the conditions are right, it should steadily grow more comprehensive and better adapted to the real world, and this in turn should make it capable of ever more effective assimilation of new experience. Such assimilation can then more and more truly be called *integration*; that is, integration into an already existing organic scheme.

In this way growth should of its own momentum lead to further growth. It will be seen how essential here is *continuity* of doing and experience. *All the way through, further integration can only be built on effective past integration.* To the extent to which the wrong kind of learning (that is, learning without doing and experiencing, without understanding and integration) intrudes into the process, continuity is broken. Thus the very power of future integration, and so of future true learning, is in some degree impaired.

(iii) We have noted how, after the first framework has been constructed and language mastered, the child spends the next three years or so in vigorously enacting his further education by exploration and experimentation, by imaginative play and expressive activities, by talk, questioning and listening. Thus he discovers new experiences, incessantly works over past ones, compares, reflects, corrects, connects, etc., etc., and by the age of 4-5 has performed miracles of real learning. Therefore planned education, when it formally starts at around 5, has but to carry on what is being so successfully achieved already. Its special contribution can only be to provide such conditions and such aid that the same great educational work can be done *better still*. All its planning must be aimed at this one thing. The child's interests are to be

35

stimulated further, his questions encouraged, and new problems, opportunities and materials put his way. He is to find help wherever he needs it, and active leadership that constantly carries him forward. The teacher's object should be to open up for him more and more paths by which both his present understanding and his powers of future integration can continue to *grow*.

If we now compare planned education in this sense with the traditional scheme of "school" as the place where children were trained in being taught, or learning "lessons", we can see how close that came to the very negation of growth. *All* its characteristic features: the buildings, classrooms, classes, enforced attention, and notions of "learning", were like a conspiracy to insulate children from everything that could help them to grow; and a conspiracy which for many was only too successful. The processes of living learning still went on to some extent outside school; but too often on a rapidly diminishing scale. Since for one thing school and "lessons" took up most of the available time, children's own growth tended to dwindle and fade away. More than this, the child's very *standards* usually suffered severe damage, because school lessons under school conditions came to be what "learning" and "education" meant for him. With the aid of the great educational reformers, we have gone some way towards changing this, anyhow in the earlier school years; but how far have we succeeded yet in getting all the underlying *wrong assumptions* out of our system?

(iv) Summing up the task of education as a Piagetian psychology would see it, we may repeat that it must above all enable the child to carry much further what he is strongly impelled to do in any case. He urgently needs to try and build up in his mind a model of his surrounding world which will allow him to *foresee* at least its main course, to be prepared for it and to move and plan freely within it. We must help him both to get this model much better organized, and also to expand it, as far as lies in him, in some of the chief directions that radiate out all round him. Some lead to what we call geography, some to history, some to the world of living things; others to the different forms and sources of energy, or to elementary particles, or to the stars; and still others to the world of human and social affairs, institutions, thoughts, feelings and imaginings. Stimuli are always acting both *on* the child and *in* him to draw him in all these directions; in the end he must decide which draw him most, but to begin with, he can become curious and interested about virtually any of them. That is the most precious first asset of the educational process. These interests should be so fostered that his world will continually enlarge all round him, whilst yet remaining one world. Such it is in very truth; education need not create or "teach" this, but only has to ensure that it is preserved. All the child's natural learning by doing, experiencing and assimilating tends that way and makes it easy to help him, however widely and variously his vision may expand. On the other hand, we can also plan to break up his "one world", and the best recipe for this is undoubtedly to force on him all the discontinuities, the separate subjects and the taught "lessons", of conventional schooling.

3. If we pass on now to our second theme, the educational bearings of Piaget's work on the growth of *structural* thinking from 4-5 years onward, this from our current "school" angle is mainly a matter of arithmetic and elementary measurement and geometry. One chief point that has become clear is that the child's mental growth in these two fields is very much of a piece, so that they need to be taken closely together. By the same token, however, there are other basic structural notions which tend to develop at the same time and on similar lines; perhaps we should also give educational attention to these, in a way we have hardly started considering yet. Something more will be said about this later on, but the first question is what Piaget's work has to offer in the field of number and space-relations.

(i) First of all, it supplies the fullest psychological confirmation for what we have already taken in and begun to practise. The child can only learn in the true sense by (a) starting from what he feels to be real problems, problems that he is interested in and *wants* to solve: (b) working on them himself and *trying* to solve them. It is not essential that he should discover them all for himself, though the more he does so, the better. There is nothing against their being raised by the teacher—as, in the case of arithmetic and measurement, they may often have to be—so long as they spring naturally out of present concrete situations and are *actively taken over by the children*. Moreover, the latter need not get very far with their own attempts at solutions provided they are "engaged" enough to make a real effort. The teacher must in fact know *when* to come in with help (usually just by some pointer towards the next step forward); not so soon that children have not had a chance to make their own contribution, nor so late that they have become discouraged and bored. Most teachers, once this aim is clear to them, can usually feel their way to the right point of intervention. In any case if they are dealing with a group, the whole enquiry is a *joint* enterprise which they are merely leading and in which all take a hand, where they can or will. Thus the children themselves will fill each other's gaps and re-stimulate one another, yet will also find individual chances of relaxing, whilst the enterprise as a whole goes ahead.

(ii) Secondly, the important things to be mastered are not the rules for getting results right—which can too easily be a mere drill effect—but the *concepts* of number, of measurement, of length and breadth and height, of areas and perimeters, etc., so that each child can understand the problem. That means getting into his mind the hang of how we arrive at numbers, or at our elementary spatial concepts, how we can join them up and what we can do with them. Most children do in fact succeed in this, usually as early as 7-8, but it seems to come to them less through teaching than through the pressures of real life, which often confront them with the simpler number and space relations and demand some rudimentary *understanding* of these. It might, however, come sooner and more easily and might develop much further, if most of our laborious and unmeaning school lessons were replaced by activities in which the children themselves wanted to find out something. The material would not only have to be concrete, but interesting to them, and the problems such that if they could not think of the answers, they would be eager to know how one *could* solve problems like that. Here Piaget's actual experimental situations, as set out in his books on Number and Space, might well prove to be highly suggestive. They are all concrete and meaningful to the child; beads to be strung into necklaces, flowers and vases to be matched to one another, sweets to be divided up between morning and afternoon, laundry to be hung up in a certain order on a line; or challenging problems about building on an island, or planning a road, or placing players in a game, etc., etc. At the same time, however, all the situations involve numerical or spatial relationships that *test* whether children have the basic idea or not.

Of course, if they are completely unready for this idea like

38

most of Piaget's 4-5 year olds, nothing can help. If, however, we look at the illuminating middle stage, a year or so on, where children are just beginning to grope towards the right solutions, we can watch how the learning steps start. Piaget records detailed discussions with some of them in which we can see how they progress, partly because they now feel puzzled by the errors and contradictions they get into, and want to find the right answers, and partly because the experimenter helps them on in various ways by questions that are hints or by creating suggestive situations. All this material richly repays study and is likely to indicate to any teacher countless further variations, both to meet the special needs of different children and to enable them all to grasp more readily the common principle, the master-idea, which is involved.

(iii) Here, however, a cautionary comment may not be out of place. It is not difficult to imagine enthusiasts hitting on the bright idea of turning the Piagetian situations to ordinary "teaching" account—or even of devising formal "play" materials based on the right relations, which the child would thus automatically be led to "learn". Clearly this might then just turn once more into mere meaningless learning-by-training. It might indeed well prove a more effective method than most past ones, and might lead to improved "results". But that would still fail to be real learning. This, as we have seen, depends upon children being able to integrate further elements into schemes in their minds which are integrated already and into which the new elements naturally and continuously *fit*. No formal material will do that, nor any situations taken out of their context for instruction's sake. Nothing will serve but what can be made meaningful to the child: that is, by being joined up with what is meaningful to him already; real felt problems, and also real felt *discoveries* about the way to solve them.

Accordingly, the Piagetian test situations can only help true education if they are made to come so alive that children will identify themselves with the problems raised by them. It may then happen that some pupils will get genuinely interested in the structural relations concerned and may wish to follow these up and to find out more about them. That indeed is the one satisfactory way in which a transition can be achieved, at least in a number of children, to real readiness for arithmetic and elementary geometry as such. Quite generally, the more successful active education is, the more strongly it should carry pupils over eventually to a true "subject" interest in various fields; and so to eager "subject" learning, which can then in turn become fruitful because genuinely integrated into their mental growth.

(iv) A word now about the other basic structural notions which Piaget has studied: movement and speed; time; physical quantities; and logical relations (like those of class inclusion or serial order, which all of us, *including children*, draw upon in our everyday reasonings). These enter only in passing into ordinary infant-school life, and several of them not by name at all. But when occasion offers, most of these ideas are *used*, however loosely, even among 4-5 year olds; and, as Piaget has demonstrated, by the age of about 7-8 the average child has achieved a good functional hold on them, at least in the easier cases. Thus he may be able to *handle* correctly notions like that of distance—rate of movement or speed—events succeeding one another or being simultaneous or overlapping—the logical relations between wider and narrower classes—and so on. If Piaget is right, these notions (always in their "*use*" aspect, not their verbal one) develop in fact at about the same time as those of number and space, because they are closely related and make up a single structure. Moreover, most of them are just as important for our practical lives as those of arithmetic or elementary geometry. Perhaps, therefore, if we think the latter worth so much attention, we might also devote some to those other ideas. Here, too, many suitable situations are set out for us in Piaget's books, and would stand at least as good a chance of holding children's interest as any "number" problem.

There are yet other basic structural ideas with which Piaget has not dealt so far, or anyway not fully. That applies, for example, to the vital notion of *causality*. This was the theme of one of his early books, written prior to his more searching techniques. It comes into his later experimental study of the first 18 months; but he has not as yet followed it through, by the same methods, from 4-5 years onward. As however the work on the first 18 months shows, this notion is even at that time one main support of the child's model of his world. And indeed it plays so controlling a part in all his subsequent thought and action that it seems to merit as much educational help as his ideas of number and space. It would in fact be specially rewarding for later *integrative* development. This, however, is too large and uncharted a theme for more

40

than passing mention. More generally, the Piagetian type of genetic-psychological approach is itself still in mid-growth, and some of its most significant educational applications may yet be to come.

However, over against the foregoing suggestions, a final qualifying word seems desirable. It has been emphasized that the various concepts here called "structural" form the *framework* for the world-model in our minds. The *filling in* of this framework is supplied by all the child's concrete activities and experiences: his learning about land, sea, air and sky, about inanimate and animate things, about humans of every kind and their affairs, and so on. The structural frame is important, but what it holds is even more so. We may still be placing too much stress on the first, above all in its more formal aspects, at the inevitable cost of the second. Therefore, even though we may need to give attention to a much wider *range* of structural ideas than we normally do, this ought to be at the expense of other formal activities, like our laborious arithmetical drill, and not of more vital things. Framework and content should develop together, each in turn helping on the other; but framework pursuits must not, in early education, become too specialized or formalized. What matters from a broad human point of view is always the child's grasp of the basic *idea*, rather than his repertory of detailed performance. The value of Piaget's work is that in each field it lays bare the structure of those basic ideas, and thus allows us to focus our educational thinking on essentials, instead of our past inessentials. Yet they are still only *framework* essentials, and must leave scope for the child's fullest filling in. Here more than ever the principle of learning by wide and varied *doing*, *understanding* and *integrating*, must govern our educational plans.

BIBLIOGRAPHY

| N. Isaacs | *New Light on Children's Ideas of Number: the work of Professor Piaget* | Ward Lock Educational |

| Evelyn Lawrence, T. R. Theakston, N. Isaacs | *Some Aspects of Piaget's Work* | National Froebel Foundation, 1955 |

| E. A. Peel | *The Pupil's Thinking* | Oldbourne Press |

Jean Piaget	*The Psychology of Intelligence*	Routledge and Kegan Paul
	The Origin of Intelligence in the Child	
	The Child's Construction of Reality	
	Play, Dreams and Imitation in Childhood	Heinemann
	The Child's Conception of Number	Routledge and Kegan Paul
(with Inhelder)	*The Child's Conception of Space*	
(with Inhelder and Szeminska)	*The Child's Conception of Geometry*	